MW01630855

Struthiomimus

Written by Frances Swan
Illustrated by Pam Mara

LIBRARY OF CONGRESS
Library of Congress
Cataloging-in-Publication Data

Swann, Frances, 1955–
Struthiomimus / by Frances Swann;
illustrated by Pam Mara.
p. cm — (Dinosaur library)
Summary: Describes a day in the life of the dinosaur known as Struthiomimus and includes information about his physical characteristics, habits, and natural environment.
ISBN 0-86592-525-9
1. Struthiomimus—Juvenile literature.
[1. Struthiomimus. 2. Dinosaurs.] I. Mara, Pamela, ill. II. Title. III. Series.
QE862.S3S93 1988
567.9'7—dc 19 88-5971
CIP
AC

Rourke Enterprises, Inc.
Vero Beach, FL 32964

Quetzalcoatlus
Parasaurolphus
Deinosuchus
Corythasaurus
Spinosaurus
Oviraptor

Struthiomimus

Struthiomimus woke with a start. A large insect had settled on his beak. He shook his head angrily and stood up.

It was very early morning. Struthiomimus stood absolutely still. He looked around him, his intelligent eyes searching for possible dangers.

The air was humid and still. The swamp was silent except for the sound of dripping foliage. Struthiomimus looked out across the shallow waters. In the distance the strange shapes of cypress trees were outlined darkly against the sky.

Still Struthiomimus remained motionless. He watched the water. Beneath a blanket of green floating ferns fish moved slowly in the brown depths. Some distance from Struthiomimus an alligator surfaced. Only its head was visible, and it looked like a log.

Struthiomimus moved away. He cut a path through the thick ferns with a quick, trotting gait. Spiders' webs sparkled with dew in the undergrowth, and birds fluttered above him in the redwood trees.

Struthiomimus was hungry now. He began to search among the giant leaves of the gunnera plants for beetles and millipedes to eat. Then, bored with these, he chased dragonflies. He darted back and forth, jaws snapping as he caught them.

A sudden movement brought Struthiomimus to a halt. A short distance away were two male Chasmosaurus. They stood facing each other, swinging their heads violently from side to side. Struthiomimus watched this display for a moment then he turned and left.

A little further on, the trees were less dense and the sun warmed Struthiomimus' back. He stopped by the side of a lake.

A Pleisiosaur was catching fish. Struthiomimus watched it throw its long neck into the water again and again.

In the mud at his feet an unwary Salamander moved toward him. Struthiomimus caught and ate it. He then turned his attention to a pile of rotting logs.

He ripped the soft wood apart with his hands, searching for insects to eat. As he did so, a shrew-like mammal darted out. Struthiomimus caught it with one quick lunge. It was a better meal than he had hoped to get.

No longer so hungry, Struthiomimus continued to explore. The closer he got to the flood plain, the thinner the forest became. Soon there were only clumps of trees in a great green expanse of cattails.

Struthiomimus moved faster now, alert and watchful. Pterosaurs circled over the plain, and he passed several Euoplocephalus peacefully eating cattail tubers. All seemed safe.

Struthiomimus could see a large herd of Centrosaurus moving slowly toward him. Suddenly they stopped. The herd formed a protective circle around their young. Struthiomimus looked about in alarm. A pack of vicious Dromaeosaurus were racing toward the Centrosaurus herd. Struthiomimus realized the Dromaeosaurus had been watching them from the trees. Terrified, he turned and ran.

Struthiomimus ran fast, his tail held stiffly behind him. His speed quickly took him out of danger. Tired, he decided to rest next to a large lake.

A herd of Corythosaurus were drinking from the clear water. Struthiomimus joined them.

Refreshed, Struthiomimus began to relax. He searched out some young shoots, and stood chewing them. Everthing around him was peaceful. He watched the dragonflies darting low over the lily pads. At the bottom of the lake he could see a Champsosaur lying in wait for passing fish.

Struthiomimus had begun to hunt for soft shelled turtles when it began raining heavily. He left the lake and headed for the cover of the trees by the river.

In the dry season the river was slow and sandy, but this was the wet season. The river was fast and deep.

Huge logs were being swept downstream, crashing together as they went. The noise was deafening. Struthiomimus pushed his way through thick ferns, keeping away from the bank. The canopy of redwood trees above him kept out the rain. Even so, the ground was wet and slippery.

Struthiomimus searched among the saplings for lizards to eat. He found only a large nest of ants, and a long-dead, half-eaten fish.

Above the roar of the river, Struthiomimus slowly became aware of a strange noise. He moved cautiously toward the bank and peered down at the foaming water. On the far side of the river was the cause of the commotion. An Albertosaurus had cornered a Parasaurolophus. The rest of its herd were fleeing into the river.

Struthiomimus watched horrified as the Albertosaurus attacked. The two animals were much the same size, but the Albertosaurus was stronger.

It sunk its great teeth into the Parasaurolophus' neck, and kicked out at the soft underbelly of its prey. Within minutes the Parasaurolophus was dead. Struthiomimus did not stay to watch further. He scrambled upward, and headed for higher ground.

The rain had stopped now. In the hardwood forest all was still. Only the sound of the birds disturbed the silence. Struthiomimus remained watchful even so.

Tall yellow tulip trees, sweetgums, proteas and yellow ginkgo trees rose above him. In their shadow grew green, shiny figs, holly and laurel.

Many of the bushes were covered with creepers, wild grape, misteltoe and honeysuckle. They made an excellent hiding place for small mammals, and Struthiomimus hunted about for them greedily. Unsuccessful, he turned his attention to the forest floor. Here he was lucky to find a whole nest of little mammals. They made a good meal.

The light was fading, and dusk would soon fall over the forest. In the twilight, a pair of Stenonychosaurus darted back and forth across the fallen leaves. They watched Struthiomimus with their large eyes as he passed.

Struthiomimus found a soft, safe spot among the lilies and ferns and settled down. The warm evening air was filled with familiar smells and sounds. In a very short time Struthiomimus was peacefully asleep.

The Skeleton of Struthiomimus

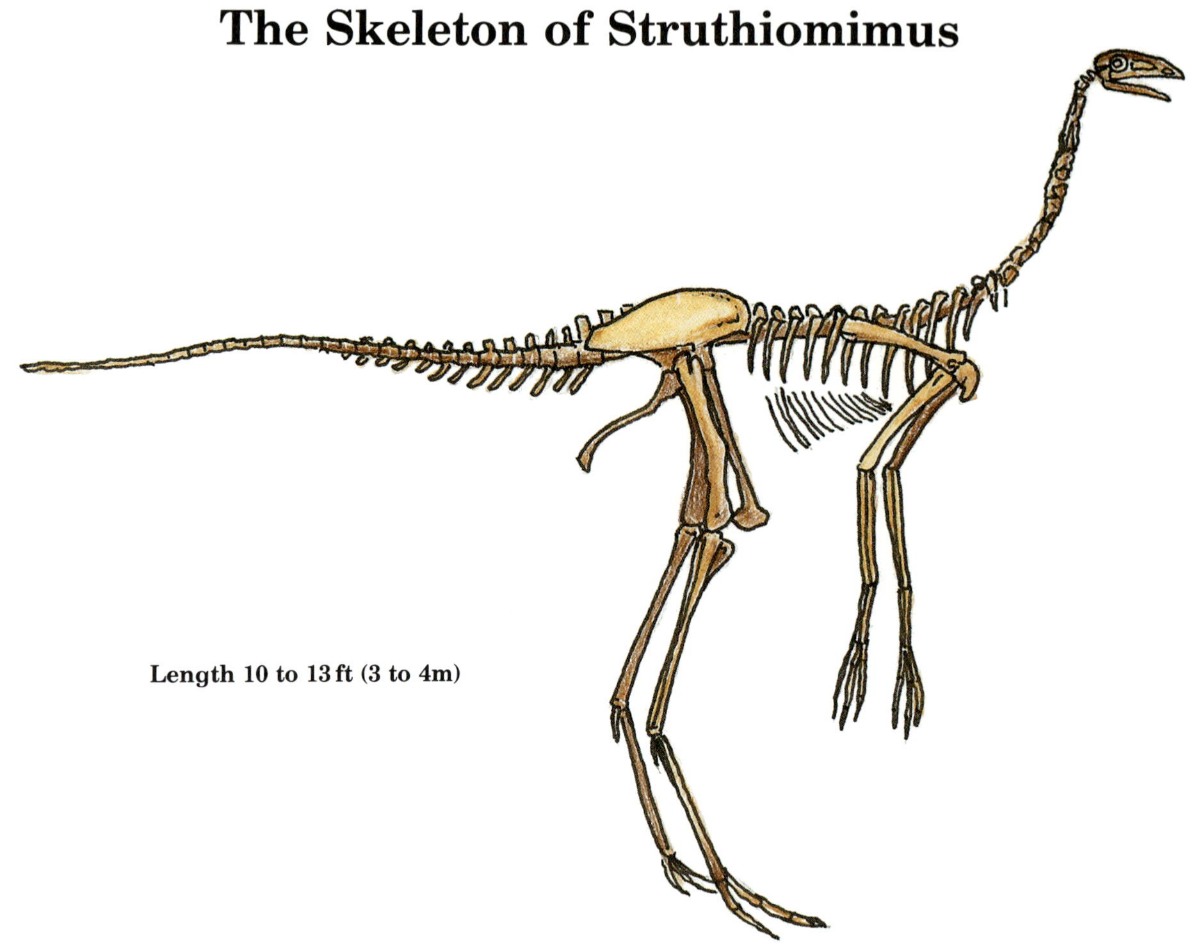

Length 10 to 13 ft (3 to 4m)

Struthiomimus and the Cretaceous World

The Age of the Dinosaurs

The word dinosaur is derived from two Greek words meaning "terrible lizard". All the dinosaurs lived in the Mesozoic era, 225 to 65 million years ago, at a time when the continents were much closer than today. At one time much of the land was one giant continent called Pangea. This great mass broke up over many millions of years, and segments drifted apart to become our present day continents.

No man has ever seen a dinosaur – man did not appear on earth until a mere 2 to 3 million years ago. So how do we know so much about the dinosaurs?

Fossil Finds

Our knowledge comes from fossils which have been discovered all over the world. Fossil skeletons, eggs, nesting sites, tracks, dung, imprints of skin, and even mummified stomach contents have been found.
New finds constantly update our view of the dinosaurs and their world.

When Struthiomimus lived

The Mesozoic age is divided into three eras – the Triassic, Jurassic and Cretaceous. Struthiomimus lived at the end of the Cretaceous era, which lasted from 136 to 65 million years. The word Cretaceous means chalk, during this time great beds of chalk were formed, and the continents took on their present shapes. At the start of the Cretaceous era the weather was mild, but by the end it was quite a lot colder.

The land was low-lying, and it was a time of high sea levels, with many deltas, rivers, lakes and swamps. Many new types of plants evolved during the Cretaceous era. Flowering plants appeared for the first time. Many of these plants would be familiar to us today.

Dinosaur Provincial Park

Fossil remains of all the animals mentioned in this book have been found along the Red Deer River in Alberta, Canada. This area is now known as Dinosaur Provincial Park.
Fossil bones, shells, wood, pollen, and leaf imprints have been found. These tell us which animals and plants lived there, and what the weather was like.
Scientists can also tell that the plains were often flooded, that the rivers were high in the wet season, and that, in the dry season, fires occurred regularly.

All about Struthiomimus

Fossil remains of Struthiomimus have been found in North America. They show that he lived between 75 and 70 million years ago Struthiomimus was a medium-sized Ornithomimosaur, or "ostrich dinosaur." These dinosaurs had many anatomical similarities to present day ostriches, and could probably run as fast. Struthiomimus had a small head on a long, mobile neck. He had no teeth, but probably a long, horny beak. The upper and lower jaw moved independently, so that food could be ground in the same way as a modern-day parrot eats.

Struthiomimus was capable of great speed. The chest, back, and lower tail were stiff. When running, the tail would be held out stiffly to counterbalance the animal's weight. Speed would have been Struthiomimus' only defence against predators. The front legs were short and slender, with three clawed fingers. The back legs were very long, with three claws similar to those of present-day running birds. Struthiomimus' diet was probably omniverous – that is, it ate both plants and animls. All the plants, insects and animals mentioned in the story were contemporary with Struthiomimus, so it would have been a varied diet.

Other Dinosaurs in this Book

CHAMOSAURUS

A 17 foot long (5.2m) long dinosaur whose remains have been found in Alberta, Canada and New Mexico. Chamosaurus had a huge, horned frill around its neck. Big skin covered "holes" in the frill reduced its weight.

EUOPLOCEPHALUS

A 20 foot (6m) long dinosaur from Alberta. Euoplocephalus was an "anklosaurid," a very heavily armored dinosaur with a tail club. Even its eyelids were made of bone.

CENTROSAURUS

A 20 foot (6m) long dinosaur from Alberta. Centrosaurus had a single nose horn, spines and horns on its neck-frill and hooves like a rhino. It was a very powerfully built dinosaur, and would probably have charged if attacked.

DROMAEOSAURUR

A 6 foot (1.8m) long dinosaur from Alberta. Only the head, arms and legs of this dinosaur have been found. It was a carnivore (meat eater) that probably hunted with others. Each hind leg had one huge claw used to disable prey.

CORYTHOSAURUS

A 33 foot long (10m) dinosaur from Alberta. Corythosaurus was a hadrosaurid dinosaur, often called a "duckbill." It had a helmet-shaped crest through which it could make a bellowing noise. Paddle-like hands indicate it could swim well to escape predators.

ALBERTOSAURUS

A 26 foot long (8m) dinosaur from Alberta and Montana. Albertosaurus was a "tyrannosaurid" – a flesh eating group. They had small foot limbs, muscular tails, and short, deep jaws with large, sharp teeth.

PARASAUROLOPHUS

A 33 foot long (10m) dinosaur from Alberta. Parasaurolophus was a hadrosaurid, or "duckbill dinosaur," like Corythosaurus. It had a very long tubular crest. It lived along the river and in marshland.

STENONYCHOSAURUS

A 6.5 foot long (2m) dinosaur from Alberta. This fast, lightly built dinosaur had a large, well developed brain. It lived on small animals, possibly mammals and lizards. Its large eyes may have helped it hunt its prey in dim light.